# BOOK 1

# Especially for Adults

## 11 Early Intermediate to Intermediate Piano Solos for Older Students

## Dennis Alexander

Over the years, my work with adult piano students has proven to be immensely rewarding and gratifying. Adults tend to be very self-motivated individuals who study piano because they love music and have always wanted to play piano, or in many cases, regret quitting piano lessons as a child. Their musical interests are different from those of children taking piano lessons. Adults need music that "warms the heart," provides opportunity for gradual technical growth and provides motivation for consistent practice.

The music in *Especially for Adults*, Book 1 is designed to accomplish all of the above. Adults will experience a real sense of accomplishment when they play these solos that contain beautiful, rich harmonies; numerous patterns that easily fit the hands; and lyrical melodies that speak to their emotions. The pieces sound sophisticated, and the titles themselves reflect this sophistication. In addition to the original music composed for this series, I have also arranged some favorite classical melodies that adults will know and enjoy.

The *Especially for Adults* series is the perfect supplement for any adult method book and will provide motivational repertoire in a variety of appealing styles for teenagers and adults of all ages. Enjoy!

*Dennis Alexander*

Day's End . . . . . . . . . . . . . . . . . . . . . . 4

Feelin' Fine . . . . . . . . . . . . . . . . . . . 14

Flamenco Fever! . . . . . . . . . . . . . . . . 6

(Theme from) Hungarian
    Rhapsody No. 2 . . . . . . . . . . . . . 22

Lost in Time . . . . . . . . . . . . . . . . . . 10

On Ol' Broadway! . . . . . . . . . . . . . . . 2

Plaisir d'amour (The Joy of Love) . . . . . . 12

Polovetsian Dance (from *Prince Igor*) . . . . 18

Reflections . . . . . . . . . . . . . . . . . . . 16

Shelby's Waltz . . . . . . . . . . . . . . . . . 20

Sneaky Kinda Rag . . . . . . . . . . . . . . . 8

*This series is dedicated to Lillian Livingston, my friend and musical colleague, who provided the motivation and inspiration for this project.*

# On Ol' Broadway!

Dennis Alexander

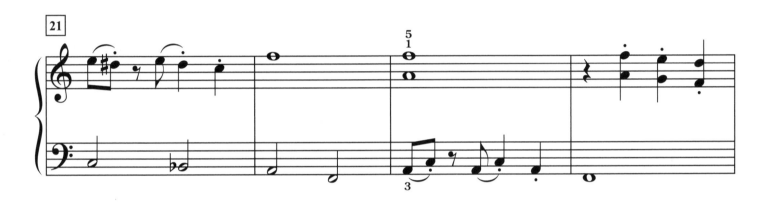

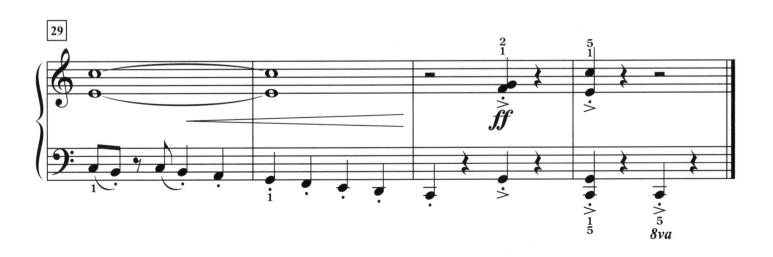

# Day's End

Dennis Alexander

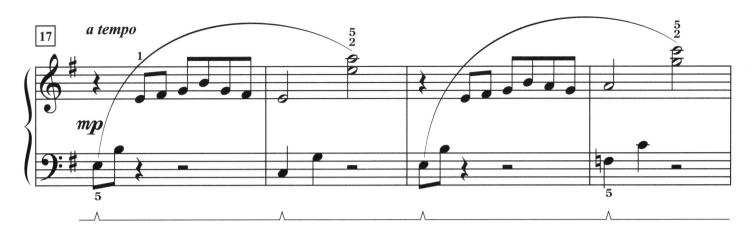

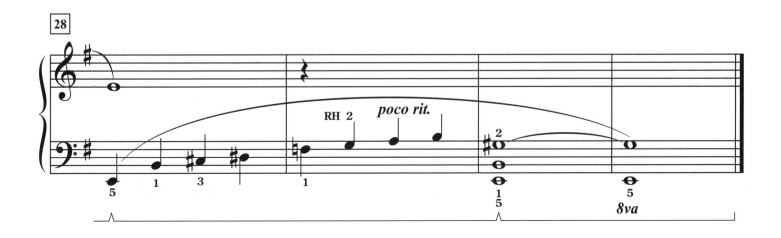

# Flamenco Fever!

Dennis Alexander

# Sneaky Kinda Rag

Dennis Alexander

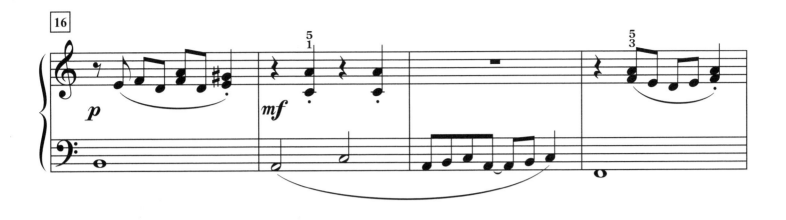

E Minor Arpeggio          E harmonic minor scale  F# + D#

EGBEGBE
RH  123 1235
LH  5 321 321

# Lost in Time

Dennis Alexander

**Andante cantabile** ($\quad$ = 112–120)

*cresc. poco a poco*

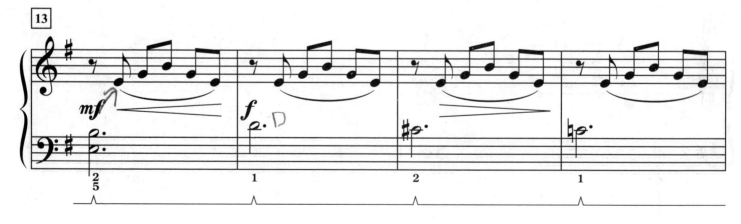

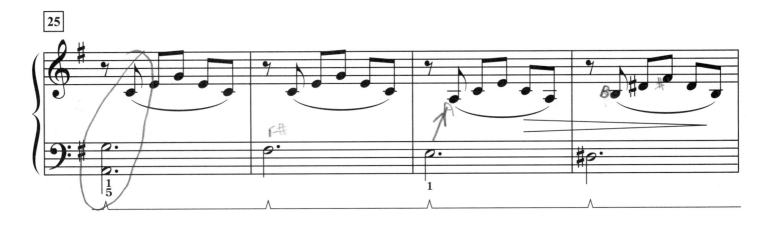

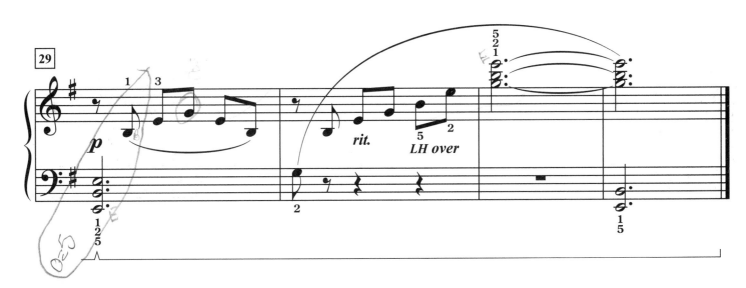

# Plaisir d'amour
## (The Joy of Love)

Giovanni Martini (1706–1784)
Arranged by Dennis Alexander

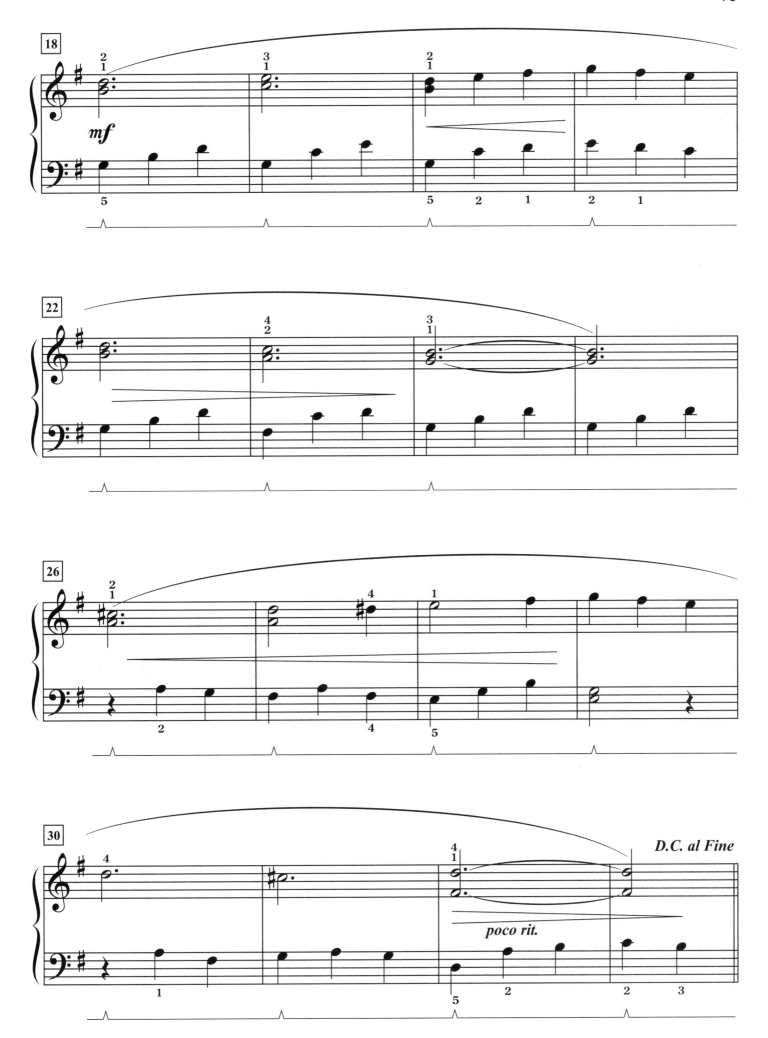

# Feelin' Fine

Dennis Alexander

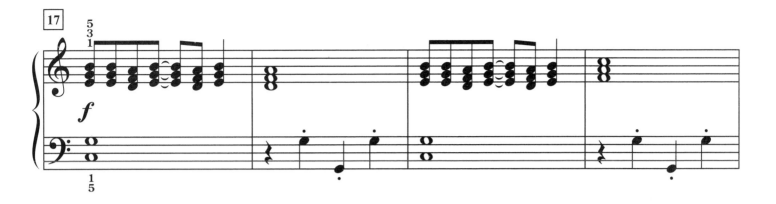

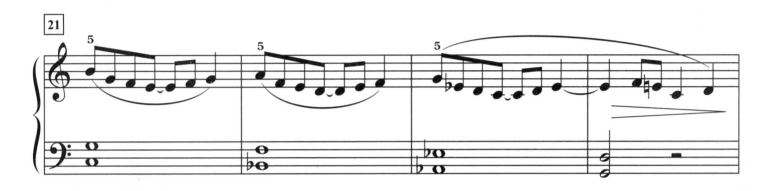

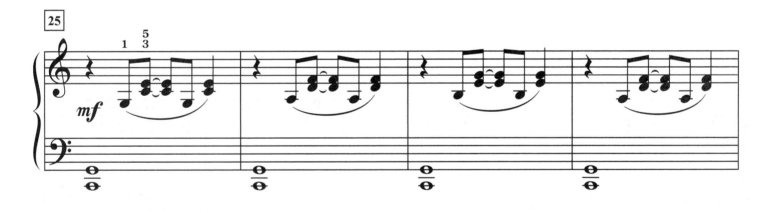

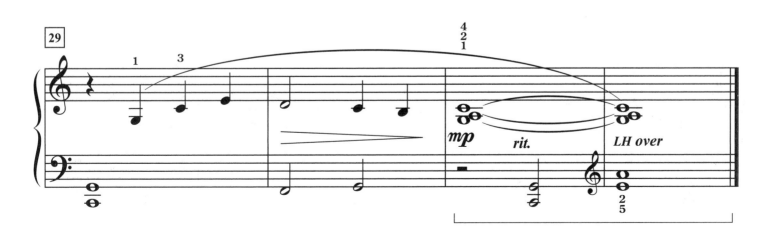

# Reflections

Dennis Alexander

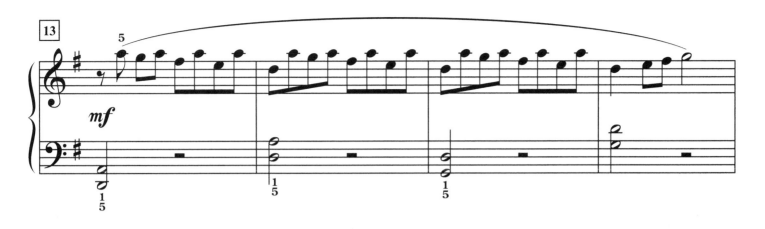

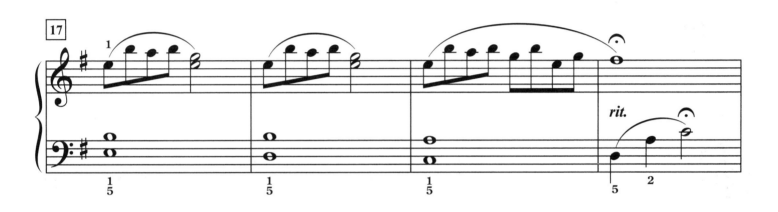

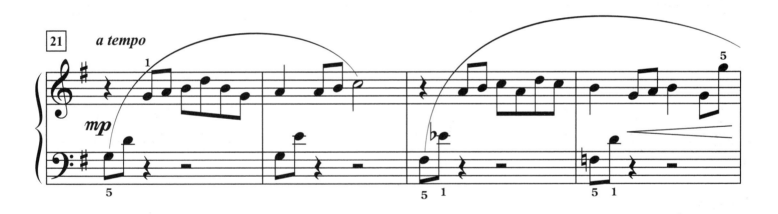

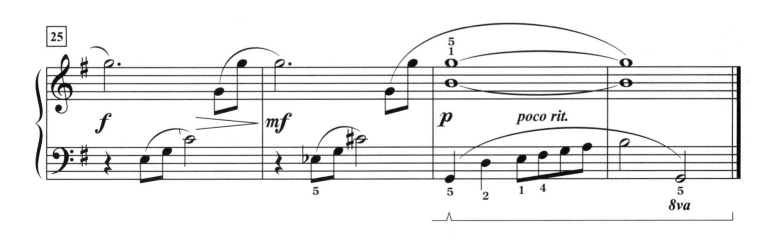

# Polovetsian Dance
## (from *Prince Igor*)

Alexander Borodin (1833–1887)
Arranged by Dennis Alexander

**Flowing** ( ♩ = 108–116)

# Shelby's Waltz

Dennis Alexander

# Theme from
# Hungarian Rhapsody No. 2

metronome ♩ = 72

Franz Liszt (1811–1886)
Arranged by Dennis Alexander

**Fast but not too fast** (♩ = 184–200)

*LH detached*

**9**  **A little faster**

**13**

*poco rit.*

*p* *gradually faster and faster to the end*

*f*

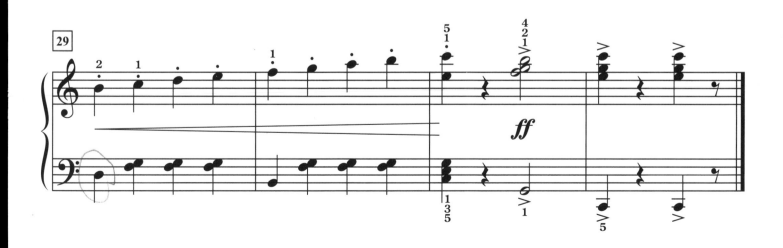

*ff*